I0412573

Roberta's Papers on the Psychology of Aging

Roberta Provenzano, PhD

iUniverse, Inc.
Bloomington

Roberta's Papers on the Psychology of Aging

Copyright © 2011 by Roberta Provenzano, PhD

All rights reserved. No part of this book may be used or reproduced by any means, graphic, electronic, or mechanical, including photocopying, recording, taping or by any information storage retrieval system without the written permission of the publisher except in the case of brief quotations embodied in critical articles and reviews.

The information, ideas, and suggestions in this book are not intended as a substitute for professional advice. Before following any suggestions contained in this book, you should consult your personal physician or mental health professional. Neither the author nor the publisher shall be liable or responsible for any loss or damage allegedly arising as a consequence of your use or application of any information or suggestions in this book.

iUniverse books may be ordered through booksellers or by contacting:

iUniverse
1663 Liberty Drive
Bloomington, IN 47403
www.iuniverse.com
1-800-Authors (1-800-288-4677)

Because of the dynamic nature of the Internet, any web addresses or links contained in this book may have changed since publication and may no longer be valid. The views expressed in this work are solely those of the author and do not necessarily reflect the views of the publisher, and the publisher hereby disclaims any responsibility for them.

Any people depicted in stock imagery provided by Thinkstock are models, and such images are being used for illustrative purposes only.

Certain stock imagery © Thinkstock.

ISBN: 978-1-4620-0712-7 (sc)
ISBN: 978-1-4620-0711-0 (dj)
ISBN: 978-1-4620-0710-3 (ebk)

Library of Congress Control Number: 2011904435

Printed in the United States of America

iUniverse rev. date: 5/16/2011

CONTENTS

FOREWORD

Roberta Provenzano was a psychologist in private practice in New York. She received her Ph.D in Psychology from the Saybrook Institute in San Francisco. She had many fields of interest, namely body/mind interrelationship, spiritual healing, psychoneuroimmunology, stress, and depression. Aging was a topic she particularly focused on in the course of her extensive research work.

The set of articles contained in the present book has been selected from documents she had kept in her filing cabinet. Looking through them, I came across unpublished papers that I read and found of publishing quality, as well as deserving recognition. I picked first those on aging because, though written in the early 1990s, the situation and arguments they develop are still very much valid today.

These articles are not only informative and well documented, but have also an advocacy potential toward the elderly, raising awareness of the aged, ageism, the prejudices associated with aging, and focus on the valuable contribution older people can offer to our society.

Since the World Assembly on Aging, held in Vienna in 1982, the topic of aging has remained on the United Nations Agenda, and their ongoing "Programme on Ageing," whose motto is "To add life to the years that have been added to life," has set up principles ensuring "that priority attention will be given to the situation of older persons ... to address the independence, participation, care, self-fulfillment, and dignity of older persons." Roberta's papers are in line with such internationally shared concerns and are therefore likely to be of interest to a diverse readership.

They are presented in this book in faithful homage to her memory.

Carmen Barthet,
Friend and Legal Representative

New York, November 8, 2010

Part One

1

Myths and Stereotypes Commonly Imposed upon the Elderly within Our Society—and Their Effects

The unfortunate position in which large numbers of elderly people find themselves is rationalized by a widely accepted view that has little scientific substantiation, maintaining that aging is synonymous with general deterioration and that the aged can contribute little if anything to our technologically advanced society.

To be sure, there are biological changes associated with normal aging, but they seldom mean that the elderly cannot deal efficiently and productively with life. Also, there are enormous individual differences in aging: some people become exceptionally disabled and require the services available to the handicapped, while many others live to a very old age in excellent physical, mental, and emotional condition. In many populations, a good deal of decline is statistically normal in the sense that it occurs frequently, but it is not developmentally normal.

Chronological age and biological age aren't necessarily one and the same, and the dominance of chronological aging is a myth. Older people are not necessarily unproductive and do tend to remain actively concerned about their personal and community relationships. In 1974, 30 percent of people over sixty-five were employed in America. Many others have become involved in community organizations and creative activities—the kind of work they had no time for while building a career and raising a family. Physiological decline in functions may not be fixed and inevitable, and there may be both behavioral and biological intervention strategies that may reverse some of the deleterious performance observed in old people. Drastic decline occurs only when development has been impaired by severe psychological, social, and biological circumstances, so normal aging and pathological aging should be differentiated. If conditions for development are reasonably favorable, old age can be an era of personal fulfillment and social contribution.

A study of a comparison (Harris 1977) between the problems attributed to most people over sixty-five by the public at large and the problems actually experienced personally by older people themselves indicated the extent to which the American public have an accurate or distorted view of what it is like to grow old.

In most cases, the discrepancy between actual experience and expectation is enormous. While serious problems of not enough money, fear of crime, poor health, loneliness, and inadequate medical care indeed exist among certain minorities of old people, they are by no means as all-pervasive as the public thinks. Neither should having a problem be confused with being a problem. Such generalizations and myths about the elderly as an economically and socially deprived group can do the old a disservice, for they confront older people with a society that sees them merely as a problem and not as part of the solution to any of society's problems. Such problems that the public perceives among the elderly can only generate a sense of guilt and pity among the young instead of a sense of appreciation toward the elderly.

A striking finding in Harris's study is the fact that age does not appear to influence significantly the way individuals tend to view themselves: the public sixty-five and over tends to see itself as somewhat more friendly and warm than those under sixty-five, and as wiser from experience. The public's view of themselves in both these areas tends to increase continually with age. The public sixty-five and over have a relatively high self-image in terms of being useful members of their community: 40 percent of them consider themselves personally to be "very useful members of their community," while 39 percent said "somewhat useful members," and 17 percent said "not useful members at all." The self-image in this area held by the public sixty-five and over is, in fact, more positive than that held by the public ages eighteen to sixty-four: while 40 percent of the older group considered themselves to be "very useful members of their community," only 29 percent of the younger group felt that way about themselves.

On the whole, the public sixty-five and over sees itself as being as bright and alert, as open-minded and adaptable, and as good at getting things done as the public eighteen to sixty-four. While the public at large may vastly underestimate the effectiveness, the open-mindedness, and the alertness of most people over sixty-five, the older public themselves have as much confidence in their own abilities as do the young and a whole lot more confidence in themselves than the public has in them.

The myth of rigidity or resistance to change is equally as suspect as all the others. The concept of rigidity is not a unitary one; a person can be rigid in one area of endeavor but not in another. Although Freud postulated that the defenses of the organism are solidly rigidified by adulthood and that there is no hope for change, several studies of both animal and human subjects— which had pointed to some difficulties in later life in maintaining flexible sets—disclosed that such difficulties disappeared or were reduced significantly when learning factors were controlled. It is true that adult character structure is remarkably stable, but ability to change depends more on previous and lifelong personality traits than on anything inherent in old age.

While the lifestyle or response patterns of the older person to his environments may appear to suggest rigidity to the casual observer, in reality they may prove to be the only way such individuals can continue to function in complex environments, namely in the case of measurable increasing decline in cognitive functioning, when there are increasing losses in visual and hearing stimuli that heretofore served to give appropriate signals to the individual as to how he might respond to his environment. In spite of these hardships, the elderly generally adapt well to increased demands, and many take on new directions through travel, learning new skills, or working in new environments.

Unquestionably, the most wide-sweeping myth in its implications is that of intellectual impairment in the elderly. Despite bodily changes related to aging, most of the older persons retain their cognitive functioning, and it has been demonstrated that intellectual decline is more related to illness and disease than to aging.

Nevertheless, portrayals of the aged persons as intellectually impaired persist and isolate them from social participation. Unable to contribute their talents, experience, and energies to society, they are stripped of the opportunities to pitch in and help solve the problems that affect our society as a whole. They begin to see themselves as passive objects manipulated by others, having lost their personal mastery and control over their environment. The loss of their sense of competence, usefulness, and involvement in the community at large is a devastating experience for the aged who attach a great importance to this role. This tends to arouse feelings of helplessness and loss of self-esteem, which in turn increase physiological stress, which seems to shock the aging organism and may well result in physical, emotional, and behavioral disorders. Some diseases such as cervical cancer, leukemia, and ulcerative colitis have been linked to feelings of hopelessness, loneliness, and isolation induced by self-defeating social practices that seem to want to ignore a large and useful human resource.

2

AGEISM AND THE PROMOTION OF AGEISM

Ageism is a systematic stereotyping of and discrimination against people because they are old, coming from a productivity-minded society placing little value on the nonproducers and stemming, among other factors, from a disguised attempt to avoid the personal realities of human aging and death. Thus, out of fear of his own mortality, the individual uses a self-protective prejudice that makes old people its victims.

Age is the most significant determinant of the negative attitudes which the young harbor toward the old. Physical changes, including getting sick, slowing down, wearing out, and showing the visible signs of age, such as wrinkles and gray hair are not a pleasant sight for the young and instill in them a deep-seated fear of growing old. In turn, when scorned by the young, the old tend to believe the negative definition applied to them and become self-conscious. They may withdraw from social events and begin to reject their own identity and reinforce what they believe to be society's rejection of them. Exaggerations of the problems of old age might force the young to struggle to look and act "young," thus inhibiting maturity and preventing them from enjoying the natural and rewarding process of aging. They may cause fears of aging that inhibit normal, rational planning for their later years.

We live in a youth-oriented culture that prizes and rewards physical vigor and youthful beauty. In its paramount preoccupation with youth, science tries to find a magical solution for the prolongation of life through embryonic cell therapy or procaine and vitamin therapy, among others. Commercial films emphasize the appeal of youth, and mass advertising sells us cosmetics and other products designed to defer the signs of aging almost as if aging were a shameful disease. It ensures that certain popular but erroneous assumptions are perpetuated in the public mind. Among other media, television shares its responsibility in perpetuating the myth of old age through stereotypic characterizations.

This clearly indicates that an effort should be made to reinforce positive images of the elderly and combat negative ones through the media.

Although the public tends to cast the blame for old age far more on the body of the older man or woman than on society's treatment of its older citizens, it would seem that society—somewhat reluctant to provide adequate services and resources to assist the aged—plays a major role in aging people by rendering them useless and isolated. Thus the picture of the elderly belonging to an institution is filtered into the public consciousness and becomes accepted. Society places a general handicap in the way of smooth adjustment in the final years of life, even when physical factors are relatively favorable. Strongly competitive societies in which too much emphasis is given to an individual's worth in terms of productive work and achievement, and in which inactivity is somewhat suspect and leisure highly commercialized (and therefore expensive), are not congenial environments in which to grow old.

3

BIOLOGICAL THEORIES OF AGING

Shock (1974) claimed that longevity is determined by a program that resides in the genes of the animal species and ultimately in the information contained in the DNA molecules of the gene. According to this theory, which is called the genetic (cellular) error theory of aging, aging and death of the cell are the result of errors that may occur at any step in the sequence of information transfer from the DNA to a different appropriate location in the cell (on the ribosomes).[1]

This transfer occurs by the assembly of RNA molecules at specific points on the DNA molecule, which then migrate to the ribosomes. It results in the formation of a protein (or enzyme) that is critical for the continued function of specific cells in the animal and that depends upon what part of the very large DNA molecule is decoded with the formation of an appropriate m-RNA.[2] The protein is not an exact copy and therefore is unable to carry out

---

1 Ribosomes are the components of cells that make proteins from all amino acids. (Wikipedia)
2 mRNA = messenger RNA: carries information about a protein sequence to the ribosomes. (Wikipedia)

its function properly. The error may be the incorporation of the wrong amino acid in the protein or a slight error in the normal sequence.

A number of limitations beset the error hypothesis; since there are many steps in the sequence of information source (DNA) and the final protein product, errors can conceivably occur at many points. Further methods will have to identify the nature of the error and the point at which it occurs. Also this theory seems to be based on a false premise because different species have different kinds of life spans, and life spans are not expandable but finite. Furthermore, the different aspects of growth and development of the organism and impact of its environment cannot be overlooked.

At the cellular level, non genetic theories of aging presume that with the passage of time, changes take place in molecules and structural elements of cells that impair their effectiveness. A non genetic theory called deprivation theory assumes that aging is due to inadequate delivery of essential nutrients and oxygen to the cells of the body and points to the increasing prevalence of atherosclerosis with advancing age and the well-known effects of vascular degeneration on cellular and tissue functions. The fact that all the cells in the area of a tissue affected by vascular disease die when the blood supply is shut off is, however, in sharp contrast to the chance distribution of cells that disappear from a tissue or organ with advancing age. Furthermore, there is no evidence for a systematic reduction in oxygen content of the blood with advancing age. Fasting blood glucose levels and amounts of other nutrients present in the blood do not fall with advancing age. Even in advanced old age, adequate supplies of oxygen and nutrients can be assumed to be available to cells and tissues of the body, except in pathological circumstances. The validity of this theory is extremely doubtful. Some experiments have shown that at least small molecules (glucose and oxygen) tend to pass through membranes more easily in tissues taken from senescent animals than those taken from the young. Senescence then could not be ascribed to cellular deprivation of essential materials.

The most tenable biological theory of aging in my view is Selye's stress adaptation theory. According to Selye, aging is the result of the accumulation over time of the effects of the stresses of living. Any stress that requires adaptation by the organism leaves a residuum of impairment from which the animal does not completely recover. These residuals, although they may be quite small with respect to specific events (such as those biologic reaction-products that block the machinery), accumulate over the life span so that ultimately the reserve capacities of the animal are exhausted.

The General Adaptation Syndrome consists of 3 stages:

1. The alarm reaction or awareness of the nonhomeostatic state: (release of ACTH[3] from the pituitary);

2. The stage of resistance or increased production of ACTH and release of corticosteroids, causing the body to return to the homeostatic state; and

3. The stage of exhaustion (due to overwhelming stress) characterized by a depletion of "adaptation energy" and resulting ultimately in death.

The general stress reaction involves virtually every organ and every chemical and psychological constituent of the human body. Thus it affects the total animal and its interaction with its external environment. At the point of exhaustion appear psycho-physiological symptoms that Selye terms "diseases of adaptation" such as: high blood pressure, heart attacks, peptic ulcers, migraine headaches, pains in the neck, some types of asthma, toxicomanias,

---

3 ACTH (adrenocorticotropic hormone): Corticothropin is one of the hormones secreted by the anterior lobe of the pituitary gland; controls the production and secretion of hormones by the adrenal cortex.

alcoholism, and excessive obesity or leanness due to abnormal dietary patterns. An ever-increasing proportion of the human population dies from the so-called wear-and-tear diseases, diseases of civilization, or degenerative diseases, which are primarily due to stress. Among all the autopsies (well over a thousand) performed by Selye, he has never seen a person who died of old age: we invariably die because one vital part has worn out too early in proportion to the rest of the body. Life, which holds our parts together, is only as strong as its weakest vital link. When this breaks—no matter which vital link it is—our parts can no longer be held together as a single living being.

Stress is one aspect of wear and tear throughout life, and the close relationship between aging and stress is particularly obvious. True age depends largely on the rate of wear and tear and on the speed of self-consumption, for life is essentially a process that gradually spends the given amount of adaptation energy we inherit from our parents. By learning more about the body's adaptation energy, the life span could probably be greatly prolonged.

4

INTELLECTUAL PERFORMANCE
OF THE ELDERLY

Intelligence is undoubtedly a very mysterious, elusive, and controversial concept. There are many kinds of intelligence and therefore there is a diversity of definitions. For our purpose, the definition used will emphasize concepts such as perception learning; reasoning; problem-solving; language; adaptation; and the capacity to integrate information, to generalize, to retain and utilize past experience, and to introspect. Wechsler defines intelligence as "the aggregate or global capacity of the individual to act purposefully, to think rationally, and to deal effectively with his environment." Many tests are used to assess the intelligence of all people: James and Conrad Army-Alpha intelligence test, the Stanford-Binet, the Wechsler Intelligence Scale for Children, and the Wechsler Adult Intelligence Scale, the latter being the one most widely used today. It comprises eleven subtests, each reflective of different, although related, aspects of intellective life.

Intelligence tests are unfair to the old for many reasons. First, it is known that these tests are suitable to measure skills in accord with the values of young, white, middle-class people. So to the extent that persons tested are not part of the majority culture as is the case of the old, and even when no impairment is detected in the old, the test may be unfair and not a true measure of intrinsic ability or intelligence. Tests that purport to measure the intelligence of older people should deal with problems indigenous to them, more related to their needs. Secondly, although the subject of age decline in intellectual performance is very controversial, the consensus is that an age decline in intellectual functions— although small—begins around fifty, sixty, or later and that speed of response and perceptual-integrative functions decline even before then. Wechsler had a very clear opinion about what happens to intelligence with age. He thought that most human abilities declined progressively, after reaching a peak somewhere between ages eighteen and twenty-five and that the peak age varied with the ability in question, but that the decline occurred in all mental measures of ability, including those employed in tests of intelligence. It seems that, when differences in intellectual organization are found in people of different ages, the differences tend to center around memory. In advanced age, much more than in earlier life, individual differences in memory ability account for the degree of success on a variety of tasks. Finally, there are a whole host of factors other than intellectual ability that might affect the old versus the young's responses to identical test items:

- Health problems and traumas. Brain states are adversely affected by cardiovascular pathology (blood pressure, arteriosclerosis) so frequent in the aged, and in turn affect the behavior adversely. A faulty circulation of the blood resulting in deprived brains may make for both KEG slowing and lower test scores.

- Sensory deprivation, such as hearing loss or impaired vision is bound to affect intellectual performance. The brain needs a certain amount of sensory input to function optimally and for this reason the old may function less efficiently. The greater the sensory loss, the poorer the performance on test scores. This may have vast consequences and sometimes responses to tests may be misconstrued as avoidance responses or lack of intelligence when they are simply due to functional physical deficiencies.

- Education is also a confounding variable. The amount of education a person has contributes more to his general intelligence than does his age. The older people tend to have had fewer years of schooling than the young, hence less language skills resulting in poorer understanding of test questions, which may be misinterpreted on the test as a lower level of intelligence.

- Lack of experience in test taking, inadequate motivation, increased rigidity, and distractibility associated with old age are other factors affecting the elderly responses to identical test items.

A final matter of concern when viewing the unfairness of intelligence tests to the old is the tendency toward cautiousness found in the elderly. Consequently, many elderly are less willing to guess test items about which they are uncertain, unless tests are set up in such a way that it is clearly to the old person's advantage to guess. Young people in most test situations tend to make many more errors of commission than omission, but the reverse is true for the elderly. Cautiousness may often be adaptive, but in this instance it may make the elderly appear less able than they actually are.

5

DISENGAGEMENT

As people grow older, the activities that characterized them in middle age become curtailed and as old age is reached, people tend to withdraw from other people and from activities. For the majority of the elderly, there is a disengagement from the social scene. At the same time, the world of people and institutions pushes them out.

Unquestionably there are changes with age that stem primarily from personal, inner sources, which affect social interactions and the whole pattern of life. Changes in health and role losses, for example, have great impact on life satisfaction. Though poor health is not necessarily associated with old age, older people in general suffer from a greater prevalence of chronic conditions, such as arthritis, rheumatism, high blood pressure, and heart disease. Unable to carry out activities that include physical movement, social contact with family and friends, participating in organizations, work, and leisure pursuits, physically impaired old people tend to seek refuge from personal failure in depression or even hypochondria. The old person, in losing his job through retirement when work was his sole interest, in losing social and financial security and in finding no good replacements for them, may find solace in the role of sick person.

Other inner factors that turn the old person inward and away from others are personality changes. As people become older, they perform in a way as to indicate introversion, seriousness, and cautiousness, a diminished intensity of energy, and lower needs for achievement. The changes with age that arise primarily from social, outer forces also affect the pattern of life.

Disengagement is a natural response in a society that meets the aged with rejection and expectation of failure, filling them with feelings of self-doubt and inadequacy and imposing on them norms and constraints. Thus set in a mold, the older people are often inhibited from going out and doing publicly what younger people are permitted to do. This accentuates or maybe creates the need for the aged to turn inward and can keep them from beneficial moderate activity.

Probably the deeper losses sustained by the aged, brought about as spouses, relatives, and friends die or children move away or abandon them, tend to make them withdraw and feel almost guilty to be alive.

An adequate physical environment for the elderly could compensate for deficits in old age and produce the positive reinforcement necessary to improve unproductive behavior in the aged who could, in turn, successfully adapt to an environment suitable for their needs. Person/environment transactional variables are significantly related to levels of positive self-regard in the elderly. The elderly cannot be expected to adapt in nursing homes filled with a very heterogeneous population. On the contrary, this tends to exacerbate the most serious problems of the aged, from a clinical, pragmatic, and aesthetic point of view. These places are not only improperly designed physically, but they overlook human needs for privacy, territoriality, and freedom of choice and may precipitate in the elderly a decrease in functional competence and self-esteem and engender a progressive stripping of their dignity.

One of the circumstances that fosters social isolation but which of itself does not account for it, is living alone. Even if they have social contacts, the old can feel socially isolated and lonely because of the lack of meaning of these contacts. It matters then a great deal for the old to have a confidant, someone with whom they can talk about themselves and their problems in order to diminish or abolish feelings of intense loneliness. The presence of such an intimate relationship would serve as a buffer against such decrements as loss of role or reduction of social interaction. Sometimes, however, the aged find it hard to develop significant new friendships, possibly because of lack of social skills. Lack of social opportunity, lack of transportation, decreased physical mobility, and sensory losses also contribute. Additional factors are the generally held negative stereotypes about older persons, which may make many younger or middle-aged persons, or even older persons themselves, shy away from new contacts with aging individuals.

Loneliness can also be a result of separation from the work role and from the social relationships intrinsic to the work role. One of the most important factors that press on the aging individual and give rise to frustration and emotional deprivation is the loss of earning power through forced retirement or reluctance of employers to hire older persons. A loss of earning power implies for a person a loss of status as breadwinner in the family; for a man, it may mean becoming dependent on his wife. In the absence of sufficient personal or family resources, the aged person may have to turn to outside assistance for support, the ultimate blow to self-esteem.

Disengagement does not occur for all in the same manner, however. There are those for whom the release from the constraints of social roles means great increase in personal freedom because retirement and later maturity release them from some very demanding early adulthood roles, such as parent or worker. These people have high self-regard and although they are withdrawn, they are content, calm, and interested in the world and enjoy a high degree of life satisfaction.

Personality organization or personality type seems to be the pivotal factor in predicting which individuals will age successfully and which will not, and adaptation is the key concept. Furthermore, patterns tend to reflect long-standing lifestyles, and consistencies rather than inconsistencies in coping styles predominate as an individual moves from middle age through old age.

There is no single social-psychological pattern by which people grow old. Persons age in ways that are consistent with their earlier life histories. It seems that given a relatively supportive social environment, older persons, like younger ones, will choose the combinations of activities that offer them the most ego involvement and that are most consonant with their long-established value patterns and self-concepts.

6

CHANGES IN PERSONALITY

Admittedly there are observable changes in late life as well as observable consistencies in adult personality. The difficulty resides in distinguishing and isolating those changes that are developmental from those that are not.

The biological, social, and psychological events that give substance and meaning to time, and not the passage of time itself, have to be considered. Age, as a concept, is synonymous with time, and time in itself cannot affect living function, behavior or otherwise. Time does not "cause" anything. It is a crude index of many events and experiences, and it is these indexed events which are "causal." Age therefore should not be used as an independent variable but since it is associated with behavior and describes it, it may be used as an explanation or predictor of it.

Which, if any, personality phenomena are more associated with age than with other variables, such as sex, health, ethnicity, level of education, or social class?

It is very hard to pinpoint which of the differences between younger and older persons are to be attributable to the effects of aging, and which to the differences between cohorts that have presumably been influenced by different social and cultural conditions and will thus perform differently on personality measures.

It might be useful to point to the theories that have been of major influence and have had the effect of deflecting attention from questions of developmental aspects of adult personality.

With the exception of Jung and Erikson, the psychoanalytic view discloses that the sense of identity established in adolescence produces consistency in behavior thereafter; that the character structure becomes fixed in early adulthood; and that while the ego becomes an increasingly important and autonomous agent of change, the essential nature of the personality remains stable.

The ego psychologists have given a central place to concepts of the self, intentionality in behavior, goal-seeking, and goal reformulation, but they have seldom led to systematic studies or theory regarding adult personality.

The social psychologists and role theorists, on the other hand, argue that there are no personality dispositions that are persistent across situations and that the personality can be defined as the sum or residue of social experiences and social roles.

Different modes of dealing with impulse life become salient with increasing age. Preoccupation with the inner life becomes greater; emotional cathexes[4] toward persons and objects in the outer world seem to decrease; there is a movement away from outer-world to inner-world orientation, an increased interiority. There also is a constriction in the ability to integrate a wide range of stimuli and in the willingness to deal with complicated and

---

4   Cathexis (*plural* cathexes) the conscious or unconscious attachment of emotional feeling and importance to a specific idea, person, or object.

challenging situations. Older men and women, in verbalizing opinions in dogmatic terms, in failing to clarify past-present or cause-effect relationships, and in using idiosyncratic and eccentric methods of communication give evidence of lessened sensitivity to the reactions of others and a lessened sense of relatedness to others.

A question that has been asked by gerontologists (namely, does the relationship between personality and adaptation remain the same throughout successive periods of adulthood?) relates to parenthood, intimacy, and the investment of oneself in the life of the few significant others. In the middle age, some issues relate to family roles as the middle-aged people become children of aged parents. Death becomes personalized as significant others are dying. Others relate to a very important psychological process: putting in order a store of memories, a sort of "life review." Also, time in a sense becomes restructured; one evaluates the time left to live, as opposed to the time since birth. Different personalities adapt differently to the task of aging and adaptation is itself part of personality. On the whole, it seems that such factors as work status, health, financial resources, and marital status are more decisive than chronological age in influencing degrees of adjustment in people who are age fifty and over. Although changes along these dimensions are themselves age associated, older people, like younger people, have differing capacities to cope with life stresses and to come to terms with their life situations, and chronological age is not the decisive factor.

Another level of personality functioning is represented by the nature and extent of the individual's interactions with others. Although there is a relatively adequate level of role performance until late life in healthy individuals of reasonably adequate financial means, a shrinkage in the social life space takes place that makes role activity and degree of ego investment in roles lower between ages fifty-five and eighty-five. Whether this general decrease in social interaction is to be interpreted as developmental is another question. First, interaction patterns are obviously not a function of personality alone, for no matter what the individual make-up is, he cannot achieve levels of social activity independent of the opportunities provided in the environment. On the other hand, interaction levels are partly a function of personality differences. Second, does the shrinkage of the social life space have developmental or inherent elements or is it to be interpreted as a responsive process? The declining levels of social interaction may be paced by the withdrawal of other persons rather than by the inner psychological withdrawal.

It seems reasonable to conclude that some changes in adult personality are to be interpreted as developmental while others are to be interpreted as the results of situational influences. Only after identifying and isolating these changes can we assess the utility of conceptual frameworks for explanation and prediction.

Part Two

7

OLD AGE AND THE
PROCESS OF AGING

Although Benjamin Franklin and Francis Bacon were among
those who anticipated the scientific method, a Belgian named
Quetelet is considered the first gerontologist (Birren 1961). Sir
Francis Galton was perhaps the next most prominent investigator
in the field of aging. After Galton, a number of individuals began
to study various aspects of aging (Minot 1961; Metchnikoff 1908;
Child 1915; Pearl 1922).

A number of significant publications dealing with the processes
of aging appeared in the 1920s. The 1930s laid the groundwork
for many of the developments in gerontology that have flourished
in the post-World War II period.

Since the 1950s, the growing awareness of the needs and
problems of the aged and the little knowledge about the aging
process have resulted in very extensive research focusing on diverse
aspects of the aging individual, such as social and psychological
adjustment, mental health, and psychomotor skills. However, there
is no general theory or unified body of knowledge on aging.

Despite this lack of theory, there is agreement that aging occurs through the complex interaction of biological, psychological, and sociological processes of change over time.

This process is thought to be synonymous with individual development and extends through life. While old age is seen as the last stage of the development of a person, there is little consensus as to the exact age at which this last stage begins, or the specific physical signs that mark its onset. There is a wide variation among individuals as to when aging begins; some look and seem old at sixty-five while others look and seem young at seventy-five. Why some age more successfully than others is not known and is the subject of a great deal of research. For practical purposes, the ages of sixty to sixty-five have been selected as the onset of aging in spite of the arbitrariness of these ages.

8

BIOLOGICAL ASPECTS OF AGING

Physiological changes are usually observed as concomitants of aging, but they do not occur with regularity in all ages or at a specific age. Some physical signs of aging are changes in physical appearance, slowing of responses, losses in motor and sensory functioning, a tendency to fatigue more rapidly, decreased energy, and some or all of these sometimes accompanied by chronic or progressive illnesses of a disabling nature. There are several current theories to account for the physical changes that come with age: none of these theories is wholly adequate but each contributes to our understanding of aging. Among these are that vital substances in the cells are exhausted, that information loss or errors in the coding of basic genetic material (DNA) of the cell prevents feeding of protein to the cell, or that, at conception, the genes are programmed and longevity is predetermined by such programming (Barrow 1971; Deyl 1968; Eisdorfer 1971; Franks 1970). The loss of cells over the life span within the organism, particularly the loss of neuron cells (the basic cell of the nervous system), it is believed, has a direct relationship to human appearance and behavior associated with growing old.

Despite bodily changes related to aging, however, such as the reduced effectiveness of perception—vision and hearing—and a gradual decrease in energy, many older persons retain functional capacities despite apparent organic decline.

9

Psychological Aspects of Aging

In the area of human personality there are secondary, biologically related changes associated with growing old, such as the changing physical appearance of the individual through coarser and more wrinkled skin, changing of hair color, cataracts on the eyes, etc. Often the appearance of the individual to himself—his "mirror" image, his self-conception, which differs from his image—may affect his mental attitude both toward himself and his relationship with others. Often the individual becomes self-conscious. He may withdraw from social events and begin to reject his own identity and reinforce what he believes to be society's rejection of him, through its emphasis on youth and physical beauty.

10

Sociological Aspects of Aging

Because the majority of persons in past centuries lived for the most part only into the fourth decade of life, and because their lives were primarily rooted in an economic system dependent upon the family as the unit of production, there was always a place for the older person in family and community life. However, with the changes occurring through urbanization and industrialization, there has been a breakdown of the family as a unit of production. With increased numbers of persons living into the later decades of life, changes have occurred in the age structure of society. Such changes have affected importantly the family and the place and role of older persons. These include the loss of child-rearing functions, the loss of a grandparent role, and the loss of work, among others. There is evidence attesting to the negative impact of "role loss" and social isolation (Lowenthal 1964).

Apparently, progressive losses of resources tend to arouse feelings of helplessness. These feelings, in turn, serve to create anxieties that the aged person tries to overcome by different methods of adjustment, many of which fail. Stress, resulting from drastic changes such as sudden loss of income, death of spouse, or relocations and dislocations of various sorts, seems to shock the aging organism and may well result in physical, emotional, and behavioral disorders (Lowenthal 1968).

In spite of a proliferation of research there is still little knowledge about the above issues, particularly about the relationship between biological and social aging and it is also not clear what changes are brought about through interrelated or independent psychological, sociological, and environmental events.

Since we have not succeeded in fully understanding aging processes, we must embark on a quest for knowledge with a more positive attitude and an open-mindedness unequalled so far. To do so, it is necessary to dispel the myths and stereotypes inculcated in the minds of the people on this subject by teaching them that growing old does not consist of a series of defeats, that one can approach life affirmatively and enjoy one's new status as well as its compensations.

11

NORMAL AGING

The biological changes associated with normal aging seldom mean that we cannot deal efficiently with life; they only mean that it may require more thought and effort to accomplish at sixty what we did without strain at thirty. Many individuals learn to adapt to biological changes by conserving their energies and using them efficiently; also many watch their health and physical functioning more closely as they get older and know that physiological changes do not mean deterioration if they keep their bodies active and their minds alert. Actual age should be measured by the old maxim "you are as old as you feel." If we throw out generally accepted negative patterns about aging, we can face our own old age with the same strength of character, vitality, and insatiable curiosity for life translated into a constant need for action as we had in youth, with the added advantage of wisdom, judiciousness, and breadth of perspective.

12

SELF-CONCEPT

Although the popular stereotypes of aging often include a shift to a more negative self-concept, about as many studies indicated that old people had positive views about themselves as indicated the converse (Kogan 1961). Riley (1968) found that older people (over fifty-five) in general appear to view themselves quite positively and are no more (and possibly less) negative or ambivalent in self-conceptions than younger people are. Although thinking of oneself as old does not necessarily reveal a negative self-image, it is interesting to note that in at least two studies, those of Jyrkila (1960) and Busse et al. (1959), the findings indicated that old people who viewed themselves as old tended to be more maladjusted or sicker than those who viewed themselves as young.

13

INTEGRITY VS. DESPAIR AND DISGUST

Erik Erikson sees the eight stages of life as defined by the special challenges to be met in each stage from childhood to old age. The final issue in his scheme is to develop a sense of ego integrity, integrity being the outcome of a mentally healthy life. Successful aging means accepting the consequences of choices made.

It is the acceptance of one's own and only life cycle and of the people who have become significant to it as something that had to be and that, by necessity, permitted of no substitutions ..., and an acceptance of the fact that one's life is one's own responsibility ... Although aware of the relativity of all the various lifestyles which have given meaning to human striving, the possessor of integrity is ready to defend the dignity of his own life style against all physical and economic threats. For he knows that an individual life is the accidental coincidence of but one life cycle with but one segment of history; and that for him all human integrity stands and falls with the one style of integrity of which he partakes. (Erikson 1959).

14

Intellectual Functioning

Despite bodily changes related to aging, most of the older persons retain their cognitive functioning. Intelligence is of particular importance in later life as the older persons must increasingly use this ability to assess, interpret, and manipulate their environment, and there is no reason to accept inevitable decrement in the life course of intelligence.

In fact, Owens (1963) reported some increment over a thirty-year period and showed that his subjects in their fifties scored higher in mental abilities than they had in their twenties. Similarly, the follow-up of the Berkeley Growth Study (Bayley 1968) showed that in midlife, adults performed better intellectually than they had as adolescents.

Birkhill and Shaie (1975) demonstrated that performance of the elderly on conventional measures of intellectual ability may be significantly attenuated by their reluctance to respond to test items about which they are uncertain, i.e., by their cautiousness, and that it can be enhanced markedly by the programming of reinforcement conditions. Thus, further support is provided for the view that ability-extraneous factors may be crucial mediators of intellectual performance of elderly people.

15

MEMORY

Everybody forgets things, but as a person gets older, these mental slips receive a lot of attention and become magnified. A number of studies on memory indicate that older persons perform less well in experiments demanding immediate short-term recall (Fraser 1958) and that speed of response seems to diminish with age (Birren and Botwinick 1955).

A study by Boone Beard (1968) explored some of the parameters of recent and stored memory after one hundred years of age and disclosed that a surprisingly large number of centenarians played bridge, chess, and checkers, kept their own financial records, did their own shopping, and even made dresses and furniture, all following steps without assistance.

16

LIFE SATISFACTION AND ADJUSTMENT TO AGING

As the stereotype suggests, satisfaction generally diminishes with age. However, Riley's (1968) studies indicate that the typical older person is not only as likely as a younger person to have a sense of adequacy and worth, but also as likely to seem content with his occupational and familial roles and the older a person is, the more nearly he seems to have come to terms with the specific conditions of his life. Neugarten, Havighurst, and Tobin (1961) found no relationship between age and life satisfaction and a longitudinal study conducted by Maddox and Eisdorfer (1962) revealed that morale did not decrease with age.

17

SOCIAL ISOLATION, DISENGAGEMENT, AND ROLE LOSS

Popular stereotypes associate social isolation with unhappiness and both with old age. A study of community residents and hospitalized older people showed, however, that lifelong isolation was not necessarily associated with mal adaptation in later life. The findings suggested that the former self rather than reference groups or individuals may increasingly become the salient yardstick for the sense of relative deprivation in old age (Chiriboga and Lowenthal 1973). There could be certain factors other than aging, such as environmental disturbances that force the individual to change his lifestyle and perhaps to disengage. Kutner and Tallmer (1969) found that disengagement among the aged can be predicted to occur as a concomitant of physical or social stress, which profoundly affects the manner in which their life pattern is redirected. It is not age that produces disengagement, but rather the impact of physical and social stress, which may be expected to increase with age. Work provides a social role, and the release from the constraints of a social role seems to be viewed as a loss, but it can also mean great increase in personal freedom because retirement and later maturity release persons from some very demanding early adulthood roles such as parent or worker. This point is emphasized by Bengston (1973).

18

"Senility"

Another widespread myth surrounding aging is the conviction that most old people are "senile." Senility, although not an actual medical term, is excessively used by doctors and laymen alike to explain the behavior of the elderly. Many of the reactive emotional responses of old people, such as depression, grief, and anxiety are conveniently labeled senile by practitioners who do not wish to spend the time and effort necessary to diagnose and treat their complaints; thus attitudes are formed that affect future practice. People of all ages can be forgetful, stubborn, confused, or unable to concentrate on simple tasks. Yet, when these traits appear in anyone over a certain age, it is attributed to senility. The fact that more and more old persons are perfectly alert and fully capable disproves the inevitability of senility with age and seems to confirm that senile behavior is in a large measure socially induced and can be created in anyone stripped of roles, purpose, economic independence, and physical well-being. Albrecht (1951) believes that more appropriate social roles and activities would retard or even eliminate some forms of "senility."

19

OTHER MYTHS

There is also the myth of unproductivity associated with old age, but this is not so. Old people tend to remain actively concerned about their personal and community relationships A number of people in every field have remained creative forces throughout life, Pablo. Picasso, Pablo. Casals, Arthur. Rubinstein, Albert. Einstein, BF Skinner, among many others. The myth of inflexibility or resistance to change is equally as suspect as all the others. It is true that adult character structure is remarkably stable, but ability to change depends more on previous and lifelong personality traits than on anything inherent in old age. Often when conservatism occurs, it derives not from aging, but from socioeconomic pressures. Older people are often forced to make adjustments more severe than many younger people realize:

- Spouses and friends dying;
- Moving to new neighborhoods, to institutions;
- Living on a reduced income.

Overall, despite these plights, they usually adapt well to increased constraints.

20

PERSONAL EXPERIENCE VS. PUBLIC EXPECTATION

As previously mentioned, Harris (1977) comparing the "very serious problems" generally attributed to most people over sixty-five and the "very serious problems" actually experienced personally by elderly people themselves, points out (as expounded in Table 1 at the end of this study) the gap between actual experience and public expectation. The net difference in most cases is tremendous, exemplifying myth and reality in the perception of Aging.

21

POTENTIAL ROLE OF THE MEDIA IN IMPROVING THE IMAGE OF OLDER PEOPLE

Television perpetuates myths of old age through stereotypic characterizations. Since the image of older people held by the public at large is a distorted one, tending to be negative and possibly damaging, it is necessary to use the media for a more positive image making.

Programs about older persons will find an audience as people learn to deal with reality and to accept not only issues about aging, but the presence of older faces and old age as attractive. A survey (Harris 1977) sampled young, middle-aged, and old age groups for their values relative to certain attributes and behaviors associated with the condition of being old. A concern with how television is being utilized was tied to this survey. The results indicated that a slim majority (51 percent) of television watchers said that they did sometimes see older people in television programs or commercials who they particularly looked up to or admired. This clearly indicates that an effort should be made to reinforce positive images of the elderly and combat negative ones through the media.

It is important to all of us to begin to change our negative attitudes toward aging. Old people are first of all people, like everyone else, with old age being a developmental stage of their lives. They must be led to understand and believe that it is possible for them to face this transformation gracefully. There are compensations to old age. Ample evidence exists indicating the high esteem in which older people were held in archaic societies; old age was considered an advantage, for it brought to the aged individual the rewards of a full life of honor, respect, authority, and even reverence from younger generations. The aging persons then must learn their new role while keeping their freedom and dignity. They must react against society's rejection and know that one does not get old when one remains intellectually alert. All those who, like famous thinkers and creators, have high and positive thoughts making them independent from social pressure and brainwash, are able to keep an exceptional perfection of mind until a very old age. If it is possible for a few, it is possible of all those who want to dedicate their lives to growth and improvement. But this requires the discipline of controlling negative thinking. Psychosomatic medicine is still in its infancy, but more and more it is recognized that the psyche is closely related to and can be the main cause for malfunction of the soma. Research may disclose one day that physiological aging is accentuated by depression, anxiety, or worry, and that mind can overcome the biological decline. The teaching that the future can be good, that age is the accumulation of wisdom and efficiency, and that no door is ever completely shut has been in the spiritual thinking of the ages. People must know that one's future is dependent upon change at the personal level, a work on one's inner self, and not on what masses of people have accepted as true.

Aware that the mind is a ceaseless source of creative ideas, they will not indulge in the fatalistic attitude of the world toward aging, and they will sense that nothing can happen to them unless it happens through them. Their consciousness is the sieve through which their experiences pass from idea to form and only an enlightenment of their consciousness will dispel the inner darkness and let the light shine through.

Conclusion

This study on the psychology of aging addresses in a scientific but easy-to-grasp way both the realities of aging and the myths of deterioration, senility, and lack of productivity attached to old age.

Through brief, concise sections, the biological, physiological, psychological, intellectual, and social aspects of aging are surveyed, highlighting the ways older people are able to cope with adverse conditions, which they are capable to overcome unless they feel rejected or driven to isolation, disengagement, or despair. The proved capacities of resilience of aged persons dispel many prejudices and stereotypes about inevitable and irreversible declines occurring with age.

Most importantly, the study underlines the prominent role the media could play to give a fairer, more accurate image of older people and contribute to change negative attitudes toward aging.

Last, but not least, Roberta's papers have the merit to set the record straight, and to raise awareness of a crucial fact of life, implying the necessity to integrate the issue of aging in all socioeconomic sectors, and to consider the needs and concerns of older persons into decision making at all levels. We are experiencing a tremendous demographic transformation requiring new and better-informed approaches to the role of aged people in society.

As stated by President Ronald Reagan in his message to the World Assembly on Aging in 1982: "Older persons must have a secure place in society. They must be given the opportunity to contribute both socially and economically. Above all, they must not be denied the dignity that comes from being wanted, needed, and respected."[5]

---

5   Ronald Reagan's message to the World Assembly on Aging, 1982, Report of the World Assembly on Aging, Vienna, 26 July to 6 August 1982, United Nations publication, sales no. E.82.I.16 (A/CONF.113/31), p. 90.

REFERENCES

Albrecht, R. 1951. "Social Roles in the Prevention of Senility." *Journal of Gerontology* 6: 380–86.

Baltes, P.B., and K. W. Schaie. 1974. "Aging and IQ: The Myth of the Twilight Years." *Psychology Today* 7: 35–40.

Barrows Jr., C. H. 1971. "The Challenge—Mechanisms of Biological Aging." *Gerontologist* 115: 5–11.

Bayley, N. 1968. "Cognition and Aging." In *Theory and Methods of Research on Aging*, edited by K. W. Schaie. Morgantown, W V: West Virginia University.

Bengston, V. 1973. "The Social Psychology of Aging." *Bobbs-Merrill Studies in Sociology Series*. New York: Bobbs-Merrill.

Birkhill, W. R. and K. W. Schaie. 1975. "The Effect of Differential Reinforcement of Cautiousness in Intellectual Performance among the Elderly." *Journal of Gerontology* 30: 578–83.

Birren, J. E. 1961. "A Brief History of the Psychology of Aging." *Gerontologist* 2: 67–77.

Birren, J. E. and J. Botwinick. 1955. "Speed of Response as a Function of Perceptual Difficulty and Age." *Journal of Gerontology* 10: 433–36.

Boone Beard, B. 1968. "Some Characteristics of Recent Memory of Centenarians." *Journal of Gerontology* 23: 23–30.

Busse, E. E., F. C. Jeffers, and W. D. Christ. 1959. "Factors in Age Awareness." Paper presented at the 4th International Congress of Gerontology, Merano, Italy.

Child, C. M. 1915. *Senescence and Rejuvenescence.* Chicago: University of Chicago Press.

Chiriboga, D. and M. F. Lowenthal. 1973. "Social Stress and Adaptation: Toward a Life-Course Perspective." In *The Psychology of Adult Development and Aging*, edited by C. Eisdorfer and M. P. Lawton. Washington, DC: American Psychological Association.

Deyl, Z. 1968. "Macromolecular Aspects of Aging." *Experimental Gerontology* 3: 91–112.

Eisdorfer, C. 1971. "Background and Theories of Aging." In *The Future of Aging and the Aged*, edited by C. L. Maddox. Atlanta: Southern Newspaper Publishers Association Foundation.

Erikson, E. 1959. "Growth and Crises of the Healthy Personality." *Psychological Issues* 1: 98.

Franks, L. M. 1970. "Cellular Aspects of Aging." *Experimental Gerontology* 4: 281–90.

Fraser, D. C. 1958. "Decay of Immediate Memory with Age." *Nature* 182: 1163.

Harris, L. and Associates, Inc. 1977. *Aging in America.* A Study for the National Council on the Aging, Inc.

Jyrkila, F. 1960. "Society and Adjustment to Old Age." In *Transactions of the Westermarck Society*. Vol. 5. Turku, Finland: Munksgaard.

Kogan, N. 1961. "Attitudes Toward Old People: The Development of a Scale and Examination of Correlates." *Journal of Abnormal and Social Psychology* 62: 44–54.

Kutner, B., and M. Tallmer. 1969. "Disengagement and the Stresses of Aging." *Journal of Gerontology* 24: 70–75.

Lowenthal, M. F. 1964. "Social Isolation and Mental Illness in Old Age." *American Sociological Review* 29: 24–70.

Lowenthal, M. F. 1968. "The Relationship between Social Factors and Mental Health in the Aged." In *Aging in the Modern Society*, edited by A. Simon and L. J. Epstein. Psychiatric Research Report 23. Washington, DC: American Psychiatric Association.

Metchnikoff, E. 1908. *The Prolongation of Life*. New York: Putman and Sons.

Minot, C. 1908. *The Problems of Age, Growth, and Death*. New York: Putman and Sons.

Maddox G., and C. Eisendorfer. 1962. "Some Correlates of Activity and Morale among the Elderly." *Social Forces* 40: 254–60.

Neugarten, B. C., R. J. Havighurst, and S. S. Tobin. 1961. "The Measurement of Life Satisfaction." *Journal of Gerontology* 16: 134–43.

Owens, W. A. 1963. "Age and Mental Abilities: A Longitudinal Study." *Genetic Psychology Monographs* 13: 223–94.

Pearl, R. 1922. *The Biology of Death*. Philadelphia: J. P. Lippincott.

Riegel, K. F., and R. M. Riegel. 1972. "Development, Drop, and Death." *Developmental Psychology* 6: 309–19.

Riley, M. W., et al. 1968. *Aging and society, Vol. I : An Inventory of Research Findings.* New York: Russell Sage Foundation.

TABLE 1

Personal Experience vs. Public Expectation: "Very Serious" Problems of Public 65 and Over Compared with "Very Serious" Problems Attributed to "Most People Over 65" By Total Public

"Very serious" problems	Personal Experience	Public Expectations	Net Difference
	Percentage of "Very serious" Problems Experienced by Public 65 and Over	Percentage of "Very Serious" Problems Attributed to "Most People over 65" by Total Public	
Fear of crime	23	50	+27
Poor health	21	51	+30
Not having enough money to live on	15	62	+47
Loneliness	12	60	+48
Not enough medical care	10	44	+34
Not enough education	8	20	+12
Not feeling needed	7	54	+47
Not enough to do to keep busy	6	37	+31
Not enough friends	5	28	+23
Not enough job opportunities	5	45	+40
Poor housing	4	35	+31
Not enough clothing	3	16	+13

www.ingramcontent.com/pod-product-compliance
Lightning Source LLC
Chambersburg PA
CBHW021256280526
45784CB00005B/2392